NOTEBOOK NO.
Continued From Notebook No.

Continued From Notebook No.

ASSIGNED TO:
Name

Date Issued

Phone

Company

Department

Address

City

State

Zip

Date

Signature

By

Email

Date Notebook Complete

Number Of Pages Filled In

Notes:

Copyright © 2017
Isometric Dot Paper
All rights reserved.
ISBN-13: 978-1979055505
ISBN-10: 1979055505

This Book Belongs To:

Name

Address

Phone

Email

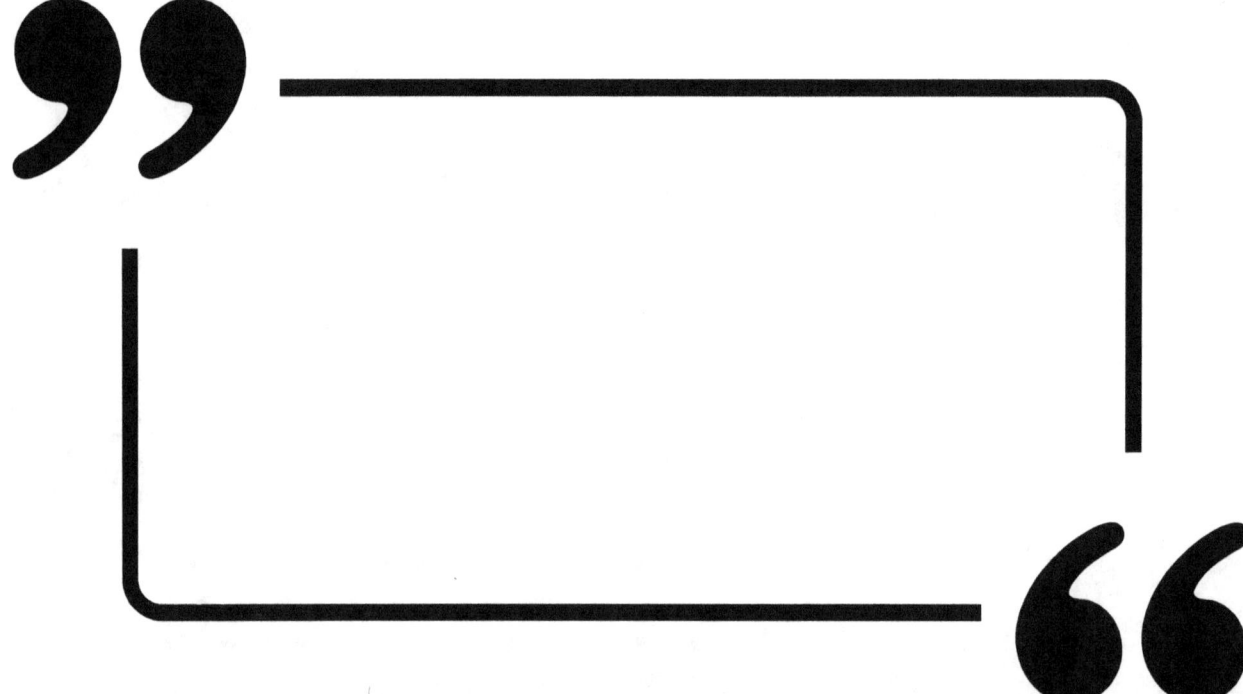

As a Reward: $

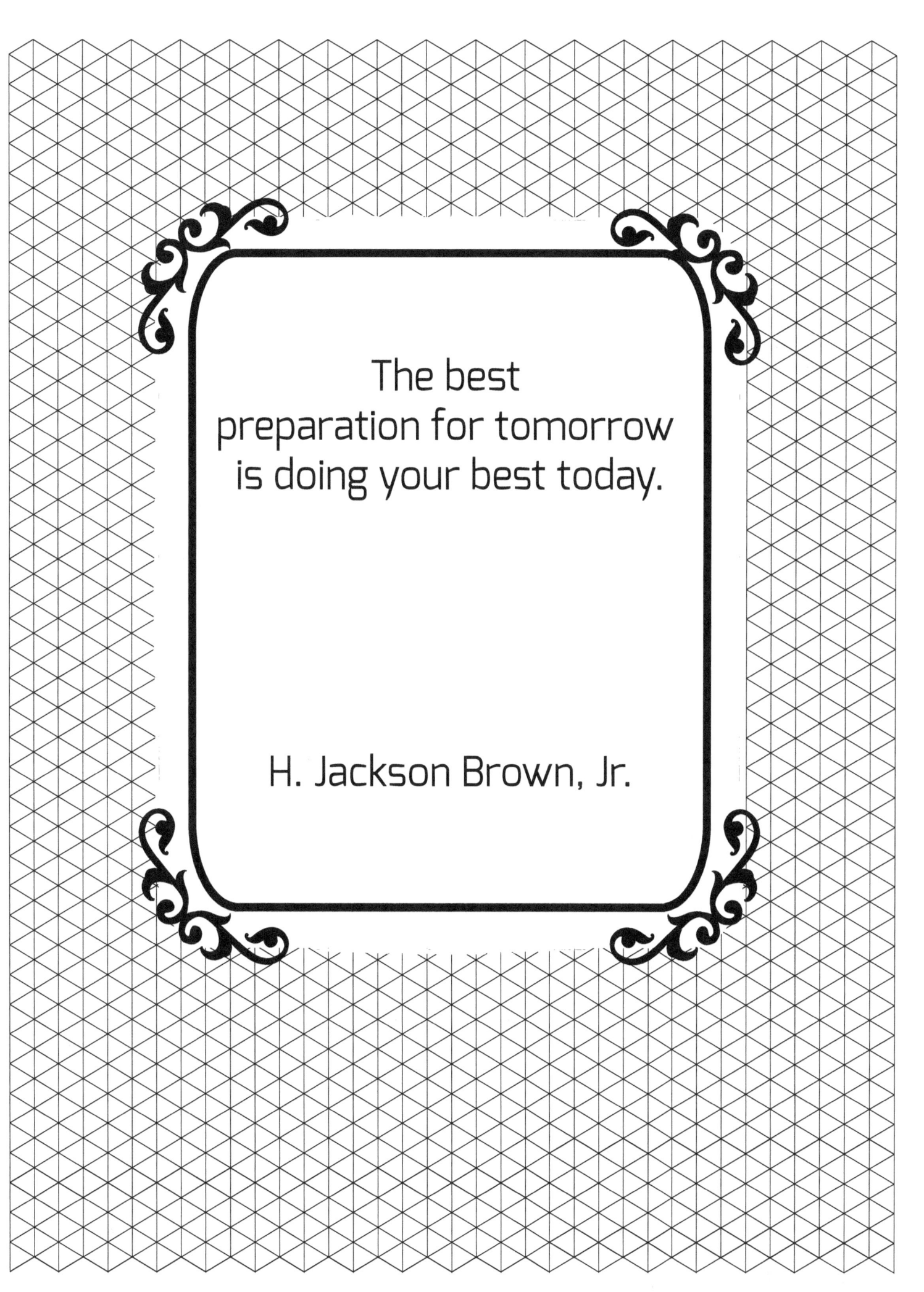

www.ingramcontent.com/pod-product-compliance
Lightning Source LLC
Chambersburg PA
CBHW082338220526
45470CB00008B/2561